ZERO E
WONDER
COOKBOOK

100+ Nourishing Recipes to Burn Fat and Boost Metabolism

FLORA VANOVER

Zero Belly Wonder Cookbook

TABLE OF CONTENTS

INTRODUCTION

Welcome to the Zero Belly Wonder Cookbook

How This Cookbook Works

The Science Behind Belly Fat and Weight Loss

The Role of Gut Health and Metabolism

Best Foods for a Zero Belly

What to Avoid: Foods That Lead to Inflammation and Weight Gain

The Importance of Hydration in Fat Loss

Meal Prepping for Success

Essential Kitchen Tools and Ingredients

How to Maintain a Zero Belly Lifestyle

CHAPTER 1: MORNING METABOLISM BOOSTERS

1. Lemon Ginger Detox Water

Ingredients:

Instructions:

Calories: 15 kcal

Cooking Tip:

2. Apple Cider Vinegar and Honey Drink

Ingredients:

Instructions:

Calories: 20 kcal

Cooking Tip:

3. Green Tea Metabolism Booster

Ingredients:

Instructions:

Calories: 5 kcal

Cooking Tip:
4. Cinnamon Honey Weight Loss Tea
  Ingredients:
  Instructions:
  Calories: 25 kcal
  Cooking Tip:
5. Cucumber and Mint Fat Flush Water
  Ingredients:
  Instructions:
  Calories: 5 kcal per cup
  Cooking Tip:
6. Chia Seed Energy Elixir
  Ingredients:
  Instructions:
  Calories: 60 kcal
  Cooking Tip:
7. Turmeric Golden Milk
  Ingredients:
  Instructions:
  Calories: 80 kcal
  Cooking Tip:
8. Aloe Vera and Lime Detox Drink
  Ingredients:
  Instructions:
  Calories: 20 kcal
  Cooking Tip:
9. Spinach and Celery Green Juice
  Ingredients:
  Instructions:

Calories: 50 kcal

Cooking Tip:

10. Fat-Burning Grapefruit Infused Water

Ingredients:

Instructions:

Calories: 10 kcal per cup

Cooking Tip:

CHAPTER 2: POWER-PACKED BREAKFASTS

1. Scrambled Egg Whites with Avocado

Ingredients:

Instructions:

Calories: 180 kcal

Cooking Tip:

2. Zero Belly Overnight Oats with Berries

Ingredients:

Instructions:

Calories: 250 kcal

Cooking Tip:

3. Blueberry Protein Pancakes

Ingredients:

Instructions:

Calories: 270 kcal

Cooking Tip:

4. Sweet Potato and Spinach Breakfast Hash

Ingredients:

Instructions:

Calories: 220 kcal

Cooking Tip:

5. High-Fiber Chia Pudding with Coconut

Ingredients:

Instructions:

Calories: 230 kcal

Cooking Tip:

6. Quinoa and Almond Breakfast Bowl

Ingredients:

Instructions:

Calories: 250 kcal

Cooking Tip:

7. Avocado and Smoked Salmon on Whole-Grain Toast

Ingredients:

Instructions:

Calories: 280 kcal

Cooking Tip:

8. Fluffy Coconut Flour Pancakes

Ingredients:

Instructions:

Calories: 260 kcal

Cooking Tip:

9. Greek Yogurt and Walnut Power Bowl

Ingredients:

Instructions:

Calories: 240 kcal

Cooking Tip:

10. Protein-Packed Banana Almond Smoothie

Ingredients:

Instructions:

Calories: 310 kcal

Cooking Tip:
CHAPTER 3: LIGHT & SATISFYING LUNCHES
1. Zesty Grilled Chicken and Kale Salad
    Ingredients:
    Instructions:
    Calories: 350 kcal
    Cooking Tip:
2. Quinoa and Black Bean Power Bowl
    Ingredients:
    Instructions:
    Calories: 320 kcal
    Cooking Tip:
3. Spicy Shrimp and Avocado Wrap
    Ingredients:
    Instructions:
    Calories: 290 kcal
    Cooking Tip:
4. Chickpea and Spinach Stuffed Peppers
    Ingredients:
    Instructions:
    Calories: 280 kcal
    Cooking Tip:
5. Mediterranean Grilled Chicken Pita
    Ingredients:
    Instructions:
    Calories: 340 kcal
    Cooking Tip:
6. Asian-Inspired Tofu and Veggie Stir-Fry
    Ingredients:

Instructions:

Calories: 270 kcal

Cooking Tip:

7. Lemon Garlic Grilled Salmon Salad

Ingredients:

Instructions:

Calories: 390 kcal

Cooking Tip:

8. Roasted Sweet Potato and Hummus Bowl

Ingredients:

Instructions:

Calories: 310 kcal

Cooking Tip:

9. Cucumber and Avocado Sushi Rolls

Ingredients:

Instructions:

Calories: 220 kcal

Cooking Tip:

10. High-Protein Lentil and Arugula Salad

Ingredients:

Instructions:

Calories: 290 kcal

Cooking Tip:

CHAPTER 4: FLAVORFUL FAT-BURNING DINNERS

1. Garlic-Lemon Grilled Chicken with Roasted Veggies

Ingredients:

Instructions:

Calories: 350 kcal

Cooking Tip:
2. Spaghetti Squash with Turkey Marinara
    Ingredients:
    Instructions:
    Calories: 320 kcal
    Cooking Tip:
3. Miso-Glazed Cod with Steamed Greens
    Ingredients:
    Instructions:
    Calories: 290 kcal
    Cooking Tip:
4. Zucchini Noodles with Pesto and Grilled Chicken
    Ingredients:
    Instructions:
    Calories: 310 kcal
    Cooking Tip:
5. One-Pan Balsamic Chicken and Brussels Sprouts
    Ingredients:
    Instructions:
    Calories: 340 kcal
    Cooking Tip:
6. Spiced Lentil and Cauliflower Curry
    Ingredients:
    Instructions:
    Calories: 320 kcal
    Cooking Tip:
7. Grilled Tofu and Quinoa Buddha Bowl
    Ingredients:
    Instructions:

Calories: 310 kcal

Cooking Tip:

8. Ginger Soy Salmon with Steamed Bok Choy

Ingredients:

Instructions:

Calories: 350 kcal

Cooking Tip:

9. Mediterranean Chickpea Stew

Ingredients:

Instructions:

Calories: 300 kcal

Cooking Tip:

10. Thai Basil Shrimp Stir-Fry

Ingredients:

Instructions:

Calories: 280 kcal

Cooking Tip:

CHAPTER 5: SATISFYING SOUPS & STEWS

1. Fat-Burning Bone Broth

Ingredients:

Instructions:

Calories: 80 kcal per cup

Cooking Tip:

2. Creamy Roasted Red Pepper Soup

Ingredients:

Instructions:

Calories: 150 kcal

Cooking Tip:

3. Hearty Lentil and Kale Stew

Ingredients:

Instructions:

Calories: 260 kcal

Cooking Tip:

4. Spicy Chicken and Black Bean Chili

Ingredients:

Instructions:

Calories: 320 kcal

Cooking Tip:

5. Coconut Ginger Carrot Soup

Ingredients:

Instructions:

Calories: 180 kcal

Cooking Tip:

6. Detox Cabbage Soup

Ingredients:

Instructions:

Calories: 120 kcal

Cooking Tip:

7. Tomato and Basil Weight-Loss Soup

Ingredients:

Instructions:

Calories: 140 kcal

Cooking Tip:

8. Broccoli and Spinach Power Soup

Ingredients:

Instructions:

Calories: 130 kcal

Cooking Tip:

9. Turmeric and Cauliflower Anti-Inflammatory Soup

Ingredients:

Instructions:

Calories: 140 kcal

Cooking Tip:

10. Chickpea and Zucchini Coconut Curry

Ingredients:

Instructions:

Calories: 280 kcal

Cooking Tip:

CHAPTER 6: GUT-HEALTHY SMOOTHIES & DRINKS

1. Green Detox Power Smoothie

Ingredients:

Instructions:

Calories: 210 kcal

Cooking Tip:

2. Metabolism-Boosting Berry Shake

Ingredients:

Instructions:

Calories: 240 kcal

Cooking Tip:

3. Anti-Inflammatory Golden Turmeric Milk

Ingredients:

Instructions:

Calories: 90 kcal

Cooking Tip:

4. Lemon-Ginger Fat Flush Water

Ingredients:

Instructions:

Calories: 10 kcal per cup

Cooking Tip:

5. Blueberry Almond Butter Shake

    Ingredients:

    Instructions:

    Calories: 280 kcal

    Cooking Tip:

6. Protein-Packed Peanut Butter Banana Smoothie

    Ingredients:

    Instructions:

    Calories: 310 kcal

    Cooking Tip:

7. Coconut Water Electrolyte Refresher

    Ingredients:

    Instructions:

    Calories: 50 kcal

    Cooking Tip:

8. Kiwi and Spinach Belly-Blast Smoothie

    Ingredients:

    Instructions:

    Calories: 220 kcal

    Cooking Tip:

9. Avocado and Cacao Energy Shake

    Ingredients:

    Instructions:

    Calories: 290 kcal

    Cooking Tip:

10. Chilled Hibiscus and Mint Tea

    Ingredients:

Instructions:

Calories: 15 kcal

Cooking Tip:

CHAPTER 7: ENERGIZING SNACKS & SMALL BITES

  1. Spicy Roasted Chickpeas

    Ingredients:

    Instructions:

    Calories: 180 kcal per ½ cup

    Cooking Tip:

  2. Nutty Trail Mix with Dark Chocolate

    Ingredients:

    Instructions:

    Calories: 250 kcal per serving

    Cooking Tip:

  3. Avocado Deviled Eggs

    Ingredients:

    Instructions:

    Calories: 220 kcal per serving

    Cooking Tip:

  4. Greek Yogurt with Cinnamon and Walnuts

    Ingredients:

    Instructions:

    Calories: 200 kcal

    Cooking Tip:

  5. No-Bake Protein Bites

    Ingredients:

    Instructions:

    Calories: 150 kcal per bite

    Cooking Tip:

6. Baked Sweet Potato Chips
    Ingredients:
    Instructions:
    Calories: 160 kcal per serving
    Cooking Tip:
7. Crunchy Kale Chips
    Ingredients:
    Instructions:
    Calories: 110 kcal per serving
    Cooking Tip:
8. Almond Butter and Apple Slices
    Ingredients:
    Instructions:
    Calories: 180 kcal
    Cooking Tip:
9. Cucumber Hummus Bites
    Ingredients:
    Instructions:
    Calories: 120 kcal
    Cooking Tip:
10. Zesty Lemon Chia Pudding
    Ingredients:
    Instructions:
    Calories: 180 kcal
    Cooking Tip:
CHAPTER 8: BELLY-FLAT DESSERTS
    1. Dark Chocolate Avocado Mousse
        Ingredients:
        Instructions:

Calories: 180 kcal per serving

Cooking Tip:

2. Baked Apple Cinnamon Crisp

Ingredients:

Instructions:

Calories: 160 kcal per serving

Cooking Tip:

3. Protein-Packed Chia Seed Pudding

Ingredients:

Instructions:

Calories: 180 kcal per serving

Cooking Tip:

4. Coconut Flour Brownies

Ingredients:

Instructions:

Calories: 220 kcal per serving

Cooking Tip:

5. Almond Butter Banana Ice Cream

Ingredients:

Instructions:

Calories: 190 kcal per serving

Cooking Tip:

6. Lemon Coconut Energy Bars

Ingredients:

Instructions:

Calories: 160 kcal per bar

Cooking Tip:

7. Blueberry Almond Crumble

Ingredients:

Instructions:

Calories: 140 kcal per serving

Cooking Tip:

8. Cinnamon-Spiced Poached Pears

Ingredients:

Instructions:

Calories: 130 kcal per serving

Cooking Tip:

9. Matcha Green Tea Frozen Yogurt

Ingredients:

Instructions:

Calories: 120 kcal per serving

Cooking Tip:

10. Honey-Sweetened Mango Sorbet

Ingredients:

Instructions:

Calories: 140 kcal per serving

Cooking Tip:

CHAPTER 9: 7-DAY ZERO BELLY MEAL PLAN

DAY 1

Morning Drink:

Breakfast:

Lunch:

Dinner:

Snack:

Dessert:

DAY 2

Morning Drink:

Breakfast:

Lunch:

Dinner:

Snack:

Dessert:

DAY 3

Morning Drink:

Breakfast:

Lunch:

Dinner:

Snack:

Dessert:

DAY 4

Morning Drink:

Breakfast:

Lunch:

Dinner:

Snack:

Dessert:

DAY 5

Morning Drink:

Breakfast:

Lunch:

Dinner:

Snack:

Dessert:

DAY 6

Morning Drink:

Breakfast:

Lunch:

Dinner:

Snack:

Dessert:

DAY 7

Morning Drink:

Breakfast:

Lunch:

Dinner:

Snack:

Dessert:

How to Follow the 7-Day Meal Plan for Maximum Results

CHAPTER 10: CONCLUSION & LONG-TERM SUCCESS STRATEGIES

1. The Zero Belly Lifestyle: A Long-Term Approach

2. How to Keep Belly Fat Off for Good

3. Meal Prep & Smart Grocery Shopping Tips

4. Simple Swaps for Everyday Eating

5. Staying on Track: Overcoming Challenges & Plateaus

6. Your Zero Belly Journey: What's Next?

CONCLUSION

BONUS: RESOURCES & FREQUENTLY ASKED QUESTIONS

INTRODUCTION

Welcome to the Zero Belly Wonder Cookbook

Welcome to *100+ Zero Belly Wonder Cookbook: Nourishing Recipes to Burn Fat and Boost Metabolism,* If you're looking for delicious, nutritious, and easy-to-make meals that help you achieve a leaner, healthier body, you're in the right place. This book isn't just about losing belly fat it's about embracing a way of eating that supports digestion, metabolism, and long-term wellness.

How This Cookbook Works

This cookbook is designed with science-backed nutrition principles to help reduce belly fat naturally. Each recipe includes:

✔ Wholesome, nutrient-dense ingredients that fight inflammation and support digestion.

✔ Balanced macronutrients (protein, fiber, and healthy fats) to keep you full and prevent cravings.

✔ Flavorful, easy-to-make meals that make healthy eating enjoyable.

✓ Options for various dietary preferences, including

vegetarian, dairy-free, and gluten-free choices.

The Science Behind Belly Fat and Weight Loss

Excess belly fat isn't just about aesthetics—it's linked to serious health conditions like heart disease, diabetes, and inflammation. The good news? By making simple food choices, you can naturally reduce visceral fat, improve digestion, and boost your metabolism. This book will help you:

- **Reduce inflammation** with anti-inflammatory superfoods.
- **Balance gut health** by consuming fiber-rich and probiotic-packed meals.
- **Boost metabolism** with thermogenic (fat-burning) ingredients.
- **Regulate blood sugar levels** with low-glycemic meals that prevent insulin spikes.

The Role of Gut Health and Metabolism

Your gut is your second brain—it controls digestion,

metabolism, and even mood and immunity. A healthy

gut microbiome helps your body absorb nutrients

efficiently and break down fat more effectively. This

cookbook prioritizes gut-friendly foods like:

✅ Fermented foods (yogurt, kimchi, sauerkraut) for probiotics.

✅ Fiber-rich vegetables (leafy greens, cruciferous vegetables, legumes) to support digestion.

✅ Prebiotic foods (garlic, onions, leeks) to nourish good bacteria in your gut.

Best Foods for a Zero Belly

To promote fat loss and optimal digestion, focus on these powerful belly-fat-fighting foods:

☐ Healthy Fats: Avocados, nuts, seeds, olive oil, coconut oil.

🍗 Lean Proteins: Chicken breast, turkey, tofu, salmon, eggs.

☐ Fiber-Rich Veggies: Kale, spinach, cauliflower, zucchini.

🍎 Low-Glycemic Fruits: Berries, apples, grapefruit.

🍚 Whole Grains: Quinoa, oats, brown rice (in moderation).

☐ Anti-Inflammatory Spices: Turmeric, ginger, cinnamon.

What to Avoid: Foods That Lead to Inflammation and Weight Gain

Avoiding processed foods and sugar-laden meals is key to reducing belly fat. Try to limit or eliminate:

⊘ Refined carbs (white bread, pasta, pastries).

⊘ Sugary drinks (soda, fruit juices with added sugar).

⊘ Processed snacks (chips, crackers, sugary cereals).

⊘ Artificial sweeteners and trans fats (margarine, hydrogenated oils).

The Importance of Hydration in Fat Loss

Water is a crucial part of weight loss. Staying hydrated flushes toxins, aids digestion, and boosts metabolism. Some of the best hydrating beverages include:

● Lemon water – promotes detox and digestion.

● Green tea – contains metabolism-boosting catechins.

☐ Cucumber-infused water – supports hydration and reduces bloating.

Meal Prepping for Success

Preparing meals in advance saves time and helps you stay on track. Here are some meal prep strategies to make healthy eating easier:

✔ Batch cooking: Cook large portions of protein and vegetables for easy meals.

✔ Pre-cut vegetables: Store chopped veggies in

containers for quick access.

✓ Portion out snacks: Keep healthy snacks like nuts and fruits ready to grab.

✓ Freeze smoothies: Blend and freeze smoothies for busy mornings.

Essential Kitchen Tools and Ingredients

Having the right tools makes healthy cooking effortless. Here are some kitchen essentials:

✐ High-quality knife set – for chopping veggies and proteins efficiently.

☉ Non-toxic nonstick pan – for easy low-oil cooking.

☐ Blender or food processor – for smoothies, soups, and sauces.

☐ Glass storage containers – for meal prep and portion control.

How to Maintain a Zero Belly Lifestyle

Healthy eating isn't a temporary diet—it's a sustainable way of life. Follow these simple habits to maintain your results:

✓ Eat balanced meals with protein, fiber, and healthy fats.

✅ Move your body daily—even a simple walk helps.

✅ Prioritize sleep—lack of sleep increases belly fat.

✅ Manage stress—chronic stress leads to weight gain.

✅ Stay consistent—progress happens with daily choices.

CHAPTER 1: MORNING METABOLISM BOOSTERS

Mornings set the tone for the rest of the day, and starting with a metabolism-boosting drink or tonic can significantly enhance fat-burning, digestion, and energy levels. This chapter includes ten powerful morning drinks designed to flush out toxins, reduce bloating, and increase calorie burn.

1. Lemon Ginger Detox Water

A refreshing and cleansing drink to jumpstart digestion and reduce bloating.

Ingredients:

- 2 cups warm water
- 1 tablespoon fresh lemon juice
- ½ teaspoon grated fresh ginger
- ¼ teaspoon cayenne pepper (optional, for extra metabolism boost)
- 1 teaspoon honey (optional)

Instructions:

1. Heat water until warm but not boiling.
2. Stir in lemon juice, ginger, cayenne pepper, and honey.
3. Let it sit for 2–3 minutes, then drink on an empty stomach.

Calories: 15 kcal

Cooking Tip:

- Use fresh lemon juice for maximum benefits.
- Adding cayenne pepper gives an **extra thermogenic boost** to help burn fat.

2. Apple Cider Vinegar and Honey Drink

Boosts digestion, stabilizes blood sugar, and supports weight loss.

Ingredients:

- 1 cup warm water
- 1 tablespoon apple cider vinegar (with the mother)
- 1 teaspoon honey
- ¼ teaspoon cinnamon (optional)

Instructions:

1. Mix all ingredients in warm water and stir well.
2. Drink first thing in the morning for best results.

Calories: 20 kcal

Cooking Tip:

- Use **raw, unfiltered apple cider vinegar** for full probiotic benefits.
- Adding cinnamon enhances **blood sugar control and digestion**.

3. Green Tea Metabolism Booster

Packed with antioxidants and catechins that help burn belly fat.

Ingredients:

- 1 cup hot water
- 1 green tea bag or 1 teaspoon loose-leaf green tea
- ½ teaspoon honey (optional)
- A squeeze of lemon

Instructions:

1. Steep green tea in hot water for 3–5 minutes.
2. Add honey and lemon if desired.
3. Drink warm, preferably before breakfast.

Calories: 5 kcal

Cooking Tip:

- Do not over-steep green tea to avoid a **bitter taste**.
- Drinking **green tea 30 minutes before exercise** enhances fat-burning effects.

4. Cinnamon Honey Weight Loss Tea

Speeds up metabolism and regulates blood sugar levels.

Ingredients:

- 1 cup hot water
- ½ teaspoon cinnamon
- 1 teaspoon honey
- 1 teaspoon lemon juice

Instructions:

1. Mix cinnamon in hot water and let it sit for 5 minutes.
2. Stir in honey and lemon juice.
3. Drink warm, preferably before breakfast.

Calories: 25 kcal

Cooking Tip:

- Ceylon cinnamon is preferred over Cassia cinnamon for its **better health benefits**.

5. Cucumber and Mint Fat Flush Water

Hydrates, reduces bloating, and helps with digestion.

Ingredients:

- 4 cups cold water
- ½ cucumber, thinly sliced
- 5 fresh mint leaves
- 1 lemon, sliced

Instructions:

1. Combine all ingredients in a pitcher and refrigerate overnight.

2. Drink throughout the day, starting in the morning.

Calories: 5 kcal per cup

Cooking Tip:

- Make a large batch and **drink throughout the day** for hydration and detox benefits.

6. Chia Seed Energy Elixir

Rich in fiber and omega-3s to keep you full and energized.

Ingredients:

- 1 cup water or coconut water
- 1 tablespoon chia seeds
- ½ teaspoon honey or maple syrup
- 1 teaspoon lemon juice

Instructions:

1. Stir chia seeds into the water and let sit for 10 minutes.
2. Add honey and lemon juice.
3. Drink before breakfast for sustained energy.

Calories: 60 kcal

Cooking Tip:

- Let the **chia seeds soak properly** to create a gel-like consistency, making digestion easier.

7. Turmeric Golden Milk

Anti-inflammatory and boosts metabolism for belly fat reduction.

Ingredients:

- 1 cup unsweetened almond milk
- ½ teaspoon turmeric powder
- ¼ teaspoon cinnamon
- 1 teaspoon honey
- A pinch of black pepper

Instructions:

1. Heat almond milk on low heat.
2. Stir in turmeric, cinnamon, and black pepper.
3. Add honey and mix well.
4. Drink warm, preferably before bed or early in the morning.

Calories: 80 kcal

Cooking Tip:

- Black pepper **enhances turmeric absorption** for better health benefits.

8. Aloe Vera and Lime Detox Drink

Soothes digestion and supports liver detoxification.

Ingredients:

- 1 cup water
- 1 tablespoon fresh aloe vera gel
- ½ teaspoon fresh lime juice
- 1 teaspoon honey (optional)

Instructions:

1. Blend aloe vera gel with water.
2. Stir in lime juice and honey.
3. Drink first thing in the morning.

Calories: 20 kcal

Cooking Tip:

- Use fresh aloe vera for **maximum gut-healing benefits**.

9. Spinach and Celery Green Juice

A nutrient-dense green juice for metabolism and digestion.

Ingredients:

- 1 cup spinach leaves
- 2 celery stalks
- ½ green apple
- 1 cup water or coconut water
- ½ teaspoon lemon juice

Instructions:

1. Blend all ingredients until smooth.
2. Strain if desired and drink fresh.

Calories: 50 kcal

Cooking Tip:

- Adding a **small green apple** balances the flavor while keeping it low in sugar.

10. Fat-Burning Grapefruit Infused Water

Loaded with vitamin C to support metabolism and fat loss.

Ingredients:

- 4 cups water
- ½ grapefruit, sliced
- ½ cucumber, sliced
- A few mint leaves

Instructions:

1. Combine all ingredients in a pitcher.
2. Let infuse for 2–4 hours in the fridge.
3. Drink throughout the morning.

Calories: 10 kcal per cup

Cooking Tip:

- **Avoid this drink if you are on certain medications**, as grapefruit can interact with them.

CHAPTER 2: POWER-PACKED BREAKFASTS

Breakfast is often called the most important meal of the day, and when it comes to burning fat and boosting metabolism, choosing the right foods can make all the difference. A high-protein, fiber-rich, and nutrient-dense breakfast helps stabilize blood sugar, curb cravings, and keep you full longer, reducing the urge to snack on unhealthy foods.

In this chapter, you'll find 10 zero belly-approved breakfasts that are delicious, easy to make, and packed with fat-burning ingredients.

1. Scrambled Egg Whites with Avocado

A high-protein, low-calorie breakfast that fuels muscle growth and keeps you full.

Ingredients:

- 4 egg whites
- 1 teaspoon olive oil
- ½ avocado, sliced

- ¼ teaspoon black pepper
- ¼ teaspoon sea salt
- 1 tablespoon chopped parsley (optional)

Instructions:

1. Heat olive oil in a pan over medium heat.
2. Add egg whites and cook while stirring gently.
3. Once cooked, season with salt and black pepper.
4. Serve with avocado slices on top.

Calories: 180 kcal

Cooking Tip:

- Adding **turmeric** to the eggs enhances anti-inflammatory benefits.

2. Zero Belly Overnight Oats with Berries

A fiber-rich, gut-friendly meal that keeps digestion on track.

Ingredients:

- ½ cup rolled oats

- ½ cup unsweetened almond milk
- ½ teaspoon chia seeds
- ½ teaspoon cinnamon
- ½ cup mixed berries (strawberries, blueberries, raspberries)
- 1 teaspoon honey or maple syrup

Instructions:

1. Mix all ingredients in a jar and stir well.
2. Refrigerate overnight.
3. Stir before serving and enjoy cold.

Calories: 250 kcal

Cooking Tip:

- Use **steel-cut oats** for an even lower glycemic impact.

3. Blueberry Protein Pancakes

A delicious high-protein breakfast without the guilt.

Ingredients:

- ½ cup oat flour
- ½ banana, mashed

- 1 egg
- ¼ cup unsweetened almond milk
- ½ teaspoon vanilla extract
- ½ teaspoon cinnamon
- ½ cup blueberries

Instructions:

1. Mix all ingredients until smooth.
2. Heat a pan over medium heat and lightly grease.
3. Pour small portions of batter and cook until bubbles form, then flip.
4. Serve with extra blueberries on top.

Calories: 270 kcal

Cooking Tip:

- Swap oat flour with **almond flour** for a low-carb option.

4. Sweet Potato and Spinach Breakfast Hash

A fiber-packed breakfast that provides slow-burning energy.

Ingredients:

- 1 medium sweet potato, diced
- 1 teaspoon olive oil
- ½ cup spinach
- ½ teaspoon garlic powder
- ¼ teaspoon black pepper
- ¼ teaspoon salt

Instructions:

1. Heat oil in a pan and sauté sweet potatoes until soft.
2. Add spinach and seasonings, cooking until spinach wilts.
3. Serve hot with a side of eggs or avocado.

Calories: 220 kcal

Cooking Tip:

- **Add a poached egg on top** for extra protein.

5. High-Fiber Chia Pudding with Coconut

A gut-healthy, anti-inflammatory breakfast loaded with omega-3s.

Ingredients:

- 1 cup unsweetened coconut milk
- 2 tablespoons chia seeds
- ½ teaspoon vanilla extract
- 1 teaspoon honey
- 2 tablespoons shredded coconut

Instructions:

1. Mix all ingredients in a jar.
2. Stir well and let sit in the fridge overnight.
3. Enjoy cold in the morning.

Calories: 230 kcal

Cooking Tip:

- Add **cinnamon** to regulate blood sugar levels.

6. Quinoa and Almond Breakfast Bowl

A protein and fiber-packed breakfast for lasting energy.

Ingredients:

- ½ cup cooked quinoa

- ½ cup unsweetened almond milk
- 1 teaspoon honey
- ¼ teaspoon cinnamon
- 2 tablespoons sliced almonds

Instructions:

1. Mix all ingredients in a bowl and stir well.
2. Serve warm or cold.

Calories: 250 kcal

Cooking Tip:

- Swap almonds with **walnuts** for more healthy fats.

7. Avocado and Smoked Salmon on Whole-Grain Toast

A heart-healthy breakfast rich in omega-3s and protein.

Ingredients:

- 1 slice whole-grain bread
- ½ avocado, mashed
- 2 ounces smoked salmon
- ¼ teaspoon black pepper

- ½ teaspoon lemon juice

Instructions:

1. Toast the bread and spread avocado on top.
2. Add smoked salmon and season with black pepper and lemon juice.

Calories: 280 kcal

Cooking Tip:

- Use **gluten-free bread** for a low-carb option.

8. Fluffy Coconut Flour Pancakes

A grain-free, low-carb pancake option for sustained energy.

Ingredients:

- ¼ cup coconut flour
- 2 eggs
- ¼ cup unsweetened almond milk
- ½ teaspoon vanilla extract
- ½ teaspoon baking powder
- ½ teaspoon cinnamon

Instructions:

1. Mix all ingredients until smooth.
2. Cook pancakes on a lightly greased pan until golden brown.

Calories: 260 kcal

Cooking Tip:

- Top with **Greek yogurt** for extra protein.

9. Greek Yogurt and Walnut Power Bowl

A simple yet powerful breakfast for gut health and fat burning.

Ingredients:

- ½ cup Greek yogurt
- 2 tablespoons walnuts, chopped
- 1 teaspoon honey
- ½ teaspoon cinnamon

Instructions:

1. Mix all ingredients in a bowl and enjoy.

Calories: 240 kcal

Cooking Tip:

- Use **full-fat Greek yogurt** for better nutrient absorption.

10. Protein-Packed Banana Almond Smoothie

A quick and easy high-protein breakfast shake.

Ingredients:

- 1 banana
- 1 scoop plant-based protein powder
- 1 cup unsweetened almond milk
- 1 tablespoon almond butter
- ½ teaspoon cinnamon

Instructions:

1. Blend all ingredients until smooth.
2. Serve immediately.

Calories: 310 kcal

Cooking Tip:

- Add **chia seeds** for extra fiber and nutrients.

CHAPTER 3: LIGHT & SATISFYING LUNCHES

A well-balanced lunch is essential for keeping energy levels high and preventing midday cravings. This chapter includes 10 light yet satisfying lunch recipes designed to fuel your body, keep blood sugar stable, and promote belly fat loss. These meals are rich in protein, fiber, and healthy fats to keep you full without feeling sluggish.

1. Zesty Grilled Chicken and Kale Salad

A protein-rich, fiber-packed salad that supports digestion and belly fat loss.

Ingredients:

- 1 grilled chicken breast, sliced
- 2 cups kale, chopped
- ½ avocado, diced
- ¼ cup cherry tomatoes, halved
- 2 tablespoons feta cheese (optional)
- 1 tablespoon olive oil
- 1 tablespoon lemon juice

- ¼ teaspoon sea salt
- ¼ teaspoon black pepper

Instructions:

1. In a bowl, massage kale with olive oil and lemon juice for 1–2 minutes to soften.
2. Add grilled chicken, avocado, cherry tomatoes, and feta cheese.
3. Season with salt and pepper, then toss to combine.

Calories: 350 kcal

Cooking Tip:

- Massaging kale **enhances its digestibility** and reduces bitterness.

2. Quinoa and Black Bean Power Bowl

A nutrient-dense, high-protein bowl to keep you full and energized.

Ingredients:

- ½ cup cooked quinoa

- ½ cup black beans, drained and rinsed
- ¼ cup corn kernels
- ¼ cup diced bell peppers
- 1 tablespoon chopped cilantro
- 1 teaspoon lime juice
- ¼ teaspoon cumin
- ¼ teaspoon sea salt

Instructions:

1. In a bowl, combine all ingredients and mix well.
2. Serve warm or chilled.

Calories: 320 kcal

Cooking Tip:

- **Add grilled shrimp or tofu** for extra protein.

3. Spicy Shrimp and Avocado Wrap

A low-carb, protein-rich wrap packed with healthy fats.

Ingredients:

- 6 medium shrimp, peeled and deveined
- ½ teaspoon paprika

- ½ teaspoon cayenne pepper
- ½ avocado, mashed
- 1 whole wheat or lettuce wrap
- ¼ cup shredded lettuce
- 1 tablespoon Greek yogurt

Instructions:

1. Season shrimp with paprika and cayenne.
2. Cook in a pan over medium heat for 3–4 minutes per side.
3. Spread mashed avocado on the wrap, then add shrimp and lettuce.
4. Drizzle with Greek yogurt, wrap tightly, and serve.

Calories: 290 kcal

Cooking Tip:

- Use **lettuce wraps** for a **low-carb, gluten-free option**.

4. Chickpea and Spinach Stuffed Peppers

A fiber-filled vegetarian meal that's easy to make.

Ingredients:

- 2 large bell peppers, halved and deseeded
- ½ cup chickpeas, mashed
- 1 cup spinach, chopped
- ¼ teaspoon garlic powder
- ¼ teaspoon black pepper
- 1 teaspoon olive oil

Instructions:

1. Preheat oven to 375°F (190°C).
2. Sauté spinach with olive oil and garlic powder for 2 minutes.
3. Mix with mashed chickpeas, then stuff mixture into bell peppers.
4. Bake for 15 minutes and serve warm.

Calories: 280 kcal

Cooking Tip:

- **Top with feta cheese** for added creaminess.

5. Mediterranean Grilled Chicken Pita

A high-protein meal packed with Mediterranean flavors.

Ingredients:

- 1 whole wheat pita
- ½ grilled chicken breast, sliced
- ¼ cup cucumber, diced
- ¼ cup cherry tomatoes, halved
- 2 tablespoons hummus
- 1 teaspoon lemon juice
- 1 teaspoon olive oil

Instructions:

1. Spread hummus inside the pita.
2. Add grilled chicken, cucumber, and cherry tomatoes.
3. Drizzle with olive oil and lemon juice.

Calories: 340 kcal

Cooking Tip:

- **Swap chicken for grilled tofu** for a plant-based alternative.

6. Asian-Inspired Tofu and Veggie Stir-Fry

A light, plant-based stir-fry with gut-friendly ingredients.

Ingredients:

- ½ cup firm tofu, cubed
- ½ cup broccoli florets
- ¼ cup carrots, sliced
- 1 teaspoon soy sauce
- ½ teaspoon sesame oil
- ½ teaspoon ginger, grated

Instructions:

1. Heat sesame oil in a pan and sauté ginger for 30 seconds.
2. Add tofu, broccoli, and carrots, cooking for 5 minutes.
3. Drizzle with soy sauce before serving.

Calories: 270 kcal

Cooking Tip:

- Use **tamari instead of soy sauce** for a gluten-free option.

7. Lemon Garlic Grilled Salmon Salad

A protein-packed salad with omega-3s for heart and brain health.

Ingredients:

- 1 grilled salmon fillet
- 2 cups mixed greens
- ½ avocado, sliced
- ¼ cup cherry tomatoes, halved
- 1 teaspoon olive oil
- 1 teaspoon lemon juice

Instructions:

1. Arrange mixed greens in a bowl.
2. Top with grilled salmon, avocado, and cherry tomatoes.
3. Drizzle with olive oil and lemon juice.

Calories: 390 kcal

Cooking Tip:

- **Marinate salmon in lemon and garlic** for extra flavor.

8. Roasted Sweet Potato and Hummus Bowl

A fiber-rich, plant-based lunch that supports digestion.

Ingredients:

- ½ cup roasted sweet potatoes, diced
- ¼ cup hummus
- ¼ cup arugula
- 1 teaspoon olive oil

Instructions:

1. Arrange roasted sweet potatoes and arugula in a bowl.
2. Add hummus and drizzle with olive oil.

Calories: 310 kcal

Cooking Tip:

- **Add grilled chicken or chickpeas** for more protein.

9. Cucumber and Avocado Sushi Rolls

A light, refreshing, and gut-friendly meal.

Ingredients:

- 1 cucumber, sliced thinly lengthwise
- ½ avocado, mashed
- ½ teaspoon sesame seeds

Instructions:

1. Spread mashed avocado on cucumber slices.
2. Roll up and sprinkle with sesame seeds.

Calories: 220 kcal

Cooking Tip:

- **Use smoked salmon inside for added protein.**

10. High-Protein Lentil and Arugula Salad

A nutrient-dense salad packed with plant-based protein.

Ingredients:

- ½ cup cooked lentils
- 2 cups arugula
- ¼ cup cherry tomatoes, halved
- 1 teaspoon balsamic vinegar
- ½ teaspoon olive oil

Instructions:

1. Toss all ingredients together in a bowl.
2. Serve fresh.

Calories: 290 kcal

Cooking Tip:

- **Add crumbled goat cheese** for extra flavor.

CHAPTER 4: FLAVORFUL FAT-BURNING DINNERS

Dinner is a crucial meal when it comes to weight management, digestion, and metabolism. Eating a nutrient-dense, high-protein, and anti-inflammatory dinner helps burn fat overnight, reduce bloating, and prevent late-night cravings.

This chapter includes 10 delicious, fat-burning dinners that are low in processed carbs, rich in fiber and protein, and packed with metabolism-boosting ingredients.

1. Garlic-Lemon Grilled Chicken with Roasted Veggies

A simple, high-protein meal with fiber-rich vegetables to aid digestion and fat loss.

Ingredients:

- 1 boneless, skinless chicken breast
- 1 teaspoon olive oil
- 1 teaspoon lemon juice

- 1 garlic clove, minced
- ½ teaspoon paprika
- ½ teaspoon black pepper
- 1 cup mixed roasted vegetables (bell peppers, zucchini, carrots)

Instructions:

1. Marinate chicken with olive oil, lemon juice, garlic, paprika, and black pepper.
2. Grill over medium heat for 5–6 minutes per side.
3. Roast mixed vegetables in the oven at 375°F (190°C) for 20 minutes.
4. Serve together.

Calories: 350 kcal

Cooking Tip:

- **Use skinless chicken breast** for leaner protein and **faster digestion**.

2. Spaghetti Squash with Turkey Marinara

A low-carb alternative to pasta that is high in fiber and protein.

Ingredients:

- ½ spaghetti squash
- ½ cup lean ground turkey
- ½ cup sugar-free marinara sauce
- 1 teaspoon olive oil
- ½ teaspoon garlic powder
- ½ teaspoon dried oregano

Instructions:

1. Roast spaghetti squash at 375°F (190°C) for 40 minutes, then scrape into noodles.
2. Sauté ground turkey with olive oil and seasonings until fully cooked.
3. Mix with marinara sauce and serve over spaghetti squash.

Calories: 320 kcal

Cooking Tip:

- **Spaghetti squash is a low-calorie alternative to pasta** that helps keep insulin levels stable.

3. Miso-Glazed Cod with Steamed Greens

A high-protein, omega-3-rich meal that boosts metabolism.

Ingredients:

- 1 cod fillet
- 1 teaspoon miso paste
- ½ teaspoon sesame oil
- 1 teaspoon lemon juice
- 1 cup steamed spinach and bok choy

Instructions:

1. Mix miso, sesame oil, and lemon juice.
2. Coat the cod fillet and bake at 375°F (190°C) for 15 minutes.
3. Serve with steamed greens.

Calories: 290 kcal

Cooking Tip:

- **Miso is packed with gut-friendly probiotics**, aiding digestion and fat metabolism.

4. Zucchini Noodles with Pesto and Grilled Chicken

A low-carb, high-fiber meal that satisfies pasta cravings.

Ingredients:

- 1 medium zucchini, spiralized
- 1 grilled chicken breast, sliced
- 1 tablespoon basil pesto
- ½ teaspoon black pepper

Instructions:

1. Sauté zucchini noodles in a pan for 2 minutes.
2. Toss with pesto and top with sliced grilled chicken.

Calories: 310 kcal

Cooking Tip:

- **Zucchini noodles are an excellent pasta substitute** with a fraction of the carbs.

5. One-Pan Balsamic Chicken and Brussels Sprouts

A delicious, fiber-rich dish to aid digestion and fight inflammation.

Ingredients:

- 1 boneless chicken breast
- 1 cup Brussels sprouts, halved
- 1 teaspoon balsamic vinegar
- 1 teaspoon olive oil
- ½ teaspoon garlic powder

Instructions:

1. Heat olive oil in a pan and sauté Brussels sprouts for 5 minutes.
2. Add chicken breast and season with garlic powder and balsamic vinegar.
3. Cook until chicken is done, about 6–7 minutes per side.

Calories: 340 kcal

Cooking Tip:

- **Brussels sprouts are rich in fiber**, keeping you full and reducing bloating.

6. Spiced Lentil and Cauliflower Curry

A plant-based dinner that is high in fiber and metabolism-boosting spices.

Ingredients:

- ½ cup lentils
- 1 cup cauliflower florets
- ½ teaspoon turmeric
- ½ teaspoon cumin
- ½ teaspoon black pepper
- 1 teaspoon olive oil

Instructions:

1. Cook lentils until soft.
2. Sauté cauliflower with olive oil and spices for 5 minutes.
3. Mix lentils and cauliflower together and serve.

Calories: 320 kcal

Cooking Tip:

- **Turmeric and black pepper work together to reduce inflammation** and enhance fat burning.

7. Grilled Tofu and Quinoa Buddha Bowl

A high-protein, plant-based meal that nourishes the body.

Ingredients:

- ½ cup cooked quinoa
- ½ cup grilled tofu, cubed
- ¼ cup diced cucumber
- 1 tablespoon tahini dressing

Instructions:

1. Arrange quinoa, tofu, and cucumber in a bowl.
2. Drizzle with tahini dressing and serve.

Calories: 310 kcal

Cooking Tip:

- **Quinoa is a complete protein**, making it perfect for plant-based eaters.

8. Ginger Soy Salmon with Steamed Bok Choy

A protein-rich, omega-3-packed meal that supports weight loss.

Ingredients:

- 1 salmon fillet
- 1 teaspoon soy sauce
- ½ teaspoon grated ginger
- 1 cup steamed bok choy

Instructions:

1. Marinate salmon with soy sauce and ginger for 10 minutes.
2. Bake at 375°F (190°C) for 12–15 minutes.
3. Serve with steamed bok choy.

Calories: 350 kcal

Cooking Tip:

- **Salmon's omega-3s help burn fat and support heart health**.

9. Mediterranean Chickpea Stew

A high-fiber, anti-inflammatory stew that supports digestion.

Ingredients:

- ½ cup chickpeas
- ½ cup diced tomatoes
- ½ teaspoon cumin
- ½ teaspoon paprika
- ½ teaspoon olive oil

Instructions:

1. Sauté chickpeas with olive oil and spices for 2 minutes.
2. Add diced tomatoes and simmer for 10 minutes.

Calories: 300 kcal

Cooking Tip:

- **Chickpeas are rich in fiber and plant-based protein**, making them perfect for fat loss.

10. Thai Basil Shrimp Stir-Fry

A light, protein-packed stir-fry that is quick and easy to make.

Ingredients:

- 6 medium shrimp
- ½ teaspoon soy sauce

- ½ teaspoon fish sauce
- 1 teaspoon olive oil
- ½ cup bell peppers, sliced
- ¼ cup basil leaves

Instructions:

1. Heat olive oil in a pan and sauté shrimp with soy sauce and fish sauce.
2. Add bell peppers and basil, cooking for 2–3 more minutes.

Calories: 280 kcal

Cooking Tip:

- **Basil helps with digestion and reduces bloating.**

CHAPTER 5: SATISFYING SOUPS & STEWS

Soups and stews are nutrient-dense, hydrating, and easy to digest, making them perfect for fat loss, gut health, and metabolism boosting. The combination of fibrous vegetables, lean proteins, and warming spices helps reduce bloating, improve digestion, and promote fullness without excess calories.

This chapter includes 10 flavorful, fat-burning soups and stews that support weight loss, immune function, and gut health while keeping you full and satisfied.

1. Fat-Burning Bone Broth

A collagen-rich broth that supports digestion and belly fat reduction.

Ingredients:

- 4 cups water
- 1 pound beef or chicken bones
- 1 tablespoon apple cider vinegar

- 1 teaspoon turmeric
- 1 teaspoon sea salt
- 2 garlic cloves, minced
- ½ teaspoon black pepper

Instructions:

1. Add all ingredients to a pot and bring to a boil.
2. Reduce heat and let simmer for 6–8 hours.
3. Strain and serve warm.

Calories: 80 kcal per cup

Cooking Tip:

- **Apple cider vinegar helps extract nutrients** from the bones for better gut health benefits.

2. Creamy Roasted Red Pepper Soup

A low-calorie, vitamin-rich soup that boosts metabolism.

Ingredients:

- 2 red bell peppers, roasted and peeled
- 1 cup vegetable broth
- ½ cup unsweetened coconut milk

- 1 teaspoon olive oil
- ½ teaspoon garlic powder
- ½ teaspoon black pepper

Instructions:

1. Blend roasted red peppers with vegetable broth until smooth.
2. Heat in a pot, adding coconut milk and seasonings.
3. Simmer for 5 minutes and serve warm.

Calories: 150 kcal

Cooking Tip:

- **Coconut milk adds healthy fats that support fat-burning.**

3. Hearty Lentil and Kale Stew

A plant-based stew packed with fiber and protein for lasting fullness.

Ingredients:

- ½ cup lentils, cooked
- 1 cup vegetable broth

- 1 cup kale, chopped
- ½ teaspoon cumin
- ½ teaspoon turmeric
- ½ teaspoon sea salt

Instructions:

1. Combine all ingredients in a pot and simmer for 15 minutes.
2. Serve warm.

Calories: 260 kcal

Cooking Tip:

- **Lentils are an excellent plant-based protein source that supports weight loss.**

4. Spicy Chicken and Black Bean Chili

A protein-packed, metabolism-boosting chili with a spicy kick.

Ingredients:

- 1 chicken breast, cooked and shredded
- ½ cup black beans

- ½ cup diced tomatoes
- 1 teaspoon chili powder
- ½ teaspoon garlic powder
- ½ teaspoon cumin

Instructions:

1. Combine all ingredients in a pot and simmer for 20 minutes.
2. Serve warm.

Calories: 320 kcal

Cooking Tip:

- **Capsaicin in chili powder boosts metabolism and fat-burning.**

5. Coconut Ginger Carrot Soup

A warming, digestion-friendly soup that supports fat loss.

Ingredients:

- 2 carrots, chopped
- 1 cup coconut milk
- 1 teaspoon grated ginger

- 1 teaspoon olive oil
- ½ teaspoon turmeric
- ½ teaspoon sea salt

Instructions:

1. Sauté carrots in olive oil until soft.
2. Blend with coconut milk and ginger until smooth.
3. Simmer for 5 minutes and serve warm.

Calories: 180 kcal

Cooking Tip:

- **Ginger helps with digestion and reduces belly bloating.**

6. Detox Cabbage Soup

A fiber-rich soup that flushes out toxins and supports weight loss.

Ingredients:

- 1 cup cabbage, chopped
- ½ cup carrots, diced
- 1 cup vegetable broth
- 1 teaspoon olive oil

- ½ teaspoon black pepper
- ½ teaspoon garlic powder

Instructions:

1. Sauté cabbage and carrots in olive oil.
2. Add vegetable broth and seasonings, then simmer for 10 minutes.

Calories: 120 kcal

Cooking Tip:

- **Cabbage supports gut health and helps eliminate excess water weight.**

7. Tomato and Basil Weight-Loss Soup

A light yet satisfying soup that supports digestion.

Ingredients:

- 2 tomatoes, diced
- 1 cup vegetable broth
- ½ teaspoon basil
- ½ teaspoon olive oil
- ¼ teaspoon black pepper

Instructions:

1. Blend tomatoes with vegetable broth until smooth.
2. Heat in a pot, adding basil and seasonings.

Calories: 140 kcal

Cooking Tip:

- **Tomatoes are rich in antioxidants that help reduce inflammation.**

8. Broccoli and Spinach Power Soup

A low-calorie, high-fiber soup that aids digestion and supports belly fat loss.

Ingredients:

- ½ cup broccoli florets
- 1 cup spinach
- 1 cup vegetable broth
- ½ teaspoon sea salt
- ½ teaspoon olive oil

Instructions:

1. Sauté broccoli and spinach in olive oil for 2 minutes.
2. Add vegetable broth and sea salt, then blend until smooth.

Calories: 130 kcal

Cooking Tip:

- **Spinach and broccoli provide fiber and essential nutrients for fat loss.**

9. Turmeric and Cauliflower Anti-Inflammatory Soup

A gut-healing, fat-burning soup that reduces inflammation.

Ingredients:

- ½ cup cauliflower florets
- 1 teaspoon turmeric
- 1 cup vegetable broth
- ½ teaspoon olive oil
- ½ teaspoon black pepper

Instructions:

1. Sauté cauliflower in olive oil for 3 minutes.
2. Add vegetable broth and turmeric, then simmer for 10 minutes.

Calories: 140 kcal

Cooking Tip:

- **Turmeric and black pepper work together to enhance fat-burning effects.**

10. Chickpea and Zucchini Coconut Curry

A protein-rich, creamy curry that aids digestion and weight loss.

Ingredients:

- ½ cup chickpeas, cooked
- ½ cup zucchini, diced
- 1 cup coconut milk
- 1 teaspoon curry powder
- ½ teaspoon garlic powder

Instructions:

1. Sauté zucchini in a pot for 2 minutes.
2. Add chickpeas, coconut milk, and seasonings.
3. Simmer for 10 minutes and serve warm.

Calories: 280 kcal

Cooking Tip:

- **Coconut milk adds healthy fats that support weight loss.**

CHAPTER 6: GUT-HEALTHY SMOOTHIES & DRINKS

Smoothies and healthy drinks can be powerful tools for boosting metabolism, improving digestion, and reducing belly fat. By combining fiber-rich fruits, gut-friendly probiotics, and anti-inflammatory ingredients, these drinks help keep you hydrated, energized, and on track with your health goals.

This chapter features 10 nutrient-dense smoothies and drinks designed to burn fat, promote gut health, and keep you full longer.

1. Green Detox Power Smoothie

A fiber-rich, digestion-friendly smoothie that fights bloating and supports weight loss.

Ingredients:

- 1 cup spinach
- ½ green apple, sliced
- 1 banana

- 1 teaspoon chia seeds
- 1 cup unsweetened almond milk
- ½ teaspoon lemon juice

Instructions:

1. Blend all ingredients until smooth.
2. Serve immediately.

Calories: 210 kcal

Cooking Tip:

- **Chia seeds add fiber that supports digestion and promotes fullness.**

2. Metabolism-Boosting Berry Shake

A high-antioxidant smoothie that reduces inflammation and speeds up metabolism.

Ingredients:

- ½ cup mixed berries (blueberries, raspberries, strawberries)
- 1 scoop plant-based protein powder
- 1 cup unsweetened almond milk

- 1 teaspoon honey
- ½ teaspoon cinnamon

Instructions:

1. Blend all ingredients until smooth.
2. Serve immediately.

Calories: 240 kcal

Cooking Tip:

- **Cinnamon helps regulate blood sugar, preventing cravings.**

3. Anti-Inflammatory Golden Turmeric Milk

A warm, gut-healing drink that reduces bloating and supports digestion.

Ingredients:

- 1 cup unsweetened almond milk
- ½ teaspoon turmeric
- ½ teaspoon cinnamon
- ½ teaspoon honey
- A pinch of black pepper

Instructions:

1. Heat almond milk on low heat.
2. Stir in turmeric, cinnamon, honey, and black pepper.
3. Serve warm.

Calories: 90 kcal

Cooking Tip:

- **Black pepper enhances turmeric absorption for maximum benefits.**

4. Lemon-Ginger Fat Flush Water

A refreshing drink that detoxifies the body and reduces bloating.

Ingredients:

- 4 cups water
- 1 lemon, sliced
- 1-inch piece of fresh ginger, sliced
- 5 fresh mint leaves

Instructions:

1. Combine all ingredients in a pitcher and refrigerate for at least 2 hours.
2. Serve chilled.

Calories: 10 kcal per cup

Cooking Tip:

- **Ginger supports digestion and speeds up metabolism.**

5. Blueberry Almond Butter Shake

A high-protein smoothie that curbs hunger and stabilizes blood sugar.

Ingredients:

- ½ cup blueberries
- 1 tablespoon almond butter
- 1 scoop protein powder
- 1 cup unsweetened coconut milk
- ½ teaspoon vanilla extract

Instructions:

1. Blend all ingredients until smooth.

2. Serve immediately.

Calories: 280 kcal

Cooking Tip:

- **Almond butter provides healthy fats that promote satiety.**

6. Protein-Packed Peanut Butter Banana Smoothie

A satisfying smoothie perfect for post-workout recovery and weight loss.

Ingredients:

- 1 banana
- 1 tablespoon peanut butter
- 1 scoop plant-based protein powder
- 1 cup unsweetened almond milk

Instructions:

1. Blend all ingredients until smooth.
2. Serve immediately.

Calories: 310 kcal

Cooking Tip:

- **Use powdered peanut butter for a lower-calorie option.**

7. Coconut Water Electrolyte Refresher

A hydrating drink that replenishes electrolytes and prevents bloating.

Ingredients:

- 1 cup coconut water
- ½ teaspoon lemon juice
- A pinch of sea salt

Instructions:

1. Stir all ingredients together.
2. Serve chilled.

Calories: 50 kcal

Cooking Tip:

- **Coconut water is naturally rich in electrolytes that prevent dehydration.**

8. Kiwi and Spinach Belly-Blast Smoothie

A digestion-friendly smoothie packed with vitamin C and fiber.

Ingredients:

- 1 kiwi, peeled
- 1 cup spinach
- ½ banana
- 1 teaspoon chia seeds
- 1 cup unsweetened coconut water

Instructions:

1. Blend all ingredients until smooth.
2. Serve immediately.

Calories: 220 kcal

Cooking Tip:

- **Kiwi is rich in digestive enzymes that help break down food.**

9. Avocado and Cacao Energy Shake

A creamy, high-fiber shake that provides lasting energy.

Ingredients:

- ½ avocado
- 1 tablespoon unsweetened cacao powder
- 1 teaspoon honey
- 1 cup unsweetened almond milk

Instructions:

1. Blend all ingredients until smooth.
2. Serve immediately.

Calories: 290 kcal

Cooking Tip:

- **Cacao powder is a natural fat burner and mood booster.**

10. Chilled Hibiscus and Mint Tea

A refreshing, metabolism-boosting herbal tea rich in antioxidants.

Ingredients:

- 1 hibiscus tea bag
- 1 cup hot water
- 1 teaspoon honey (optional)
- 5 fresh mint leaves

Instructions:

1. Steep hibiscus tea in hot water for 5 minutes.
2. Add mint leaves and let cool.
3. Serve chilled.

Calories: 15 kcal

Cooking Tip:

- **Hibiscus tea helps reduce bloating and balance blood sugar levels.**

CHAPTER 7: ENERGIZING SNACKS & SMALL BITES

Healthy snacks are essential for maintaining energy levels, preventing cravings, and keeping your metabolism active between meals. The right snacks should be nutrient-dense, high in protein and fiber, and low in processed sugars to support fat loss and gut health.

This chapter features 10 easy, satisfying, and metabolism-boosting snacks that will keep you full and energized without adding unnecessary calories.

1. Spicy Roasted Chickpeas

A crunchy, high-fiber snack that keeps you full and satisfied.

Ingredients:

- 1 cup canned chickpeas, drained and rinsed
- 1 teaspoon olive oil
- ½ teaspoon paprika

- ½ teaspoon cayenne pepper
- ¼ teaspoon sea salt

Instructions:

1. Preheat oven to 375°F (190°C).
2. Toss chickpeas with olive oil and seasonings.
3. Spread on a baking sheet and roast for 20–25 minutes.
4. Let cool before serving.

Calories: 180 kcal per ½ cup

Cooking Tip:

- **Store in an airtight container** for up to 5 days for an easy grab-and-go snack.

2. Nutty Trail Mix with Dark Chocolate

A protein-packed snack that curbs cravings while promoting fat loss.

Ingredients:

- ¼ cup almonds
- ¼ cup walnuts

- 2 tablespoons unsweetened dark chocolate chips
- 1 tablespoon sunflower seeds

Instructions:

1. Mix all ingredients together and store in a small container.
2. Enjoy as a quick, nutrient-dense snack.

Calories: 250 kcal per serving

Cooking Tip:

- **Use raw, unsalted nuts** for maximum health benefits.

3. Avocado Deviled Eggs

A protein-rich, satisfying snack that promotes fullness.

Ingredients:

- 2 hard-boiled eggs
- ½ avocado, mashed
- ¼ teaspoon black pepper
- ½ teaspoon lemon juice

Instructions:

1. Slice eggs in half and remove yolks.
2. Mash yolks with avocado, black pepper, and lemon juice.
3. Spoon mixture back into egg whites and serve.

Calories: 220 kcal per serving

Cooking Tip:

- **Avocado adds healthy fats** that keep you full longer.

4. Greek Yogurt with Cinnamon and Walnuts

A gut-friendly, protein-packed snack for digestion and metabolism.

Ingredients:

- ½ cup Greek yogurt
- 1 tablespoon chopped walnuts
- ½ teaspoon cinnamon

Instructions:

1. Mix all ingredients together and enjoy.

Calories: 200 kcal

Cooking Tip:

- **Use full-fat Greek yogurt** for better nutrient absorption.

5. No-Bake Protein Bites

A nutrient-dense snack loaded with protein, fiber, and healthy fats.

Ingredients:

- ½ cup rolled oats
- 2 tablespoons almond butter
- 1 tablespoon honey
- 1 tablespoon flaxseeds
- 1 teaspoon vanilla extract

Instructions:

1. Mix all ingredients in a bowl.
2. Roll into small balls and refrigerate for 30 minutes before serving.

Calories: 150 kcal per bite

Cooking Tip:

- **Store in the fridge for up to a week** for a quick snack option.

6. Baked Sweet Potato Chips

A crunchy, fiber-rich alternative to traditional potato chips.

Ingredients:

- 1 medium sweet potato, thinly sliced
- 1 teaspoon olive oil
- ½ teaspoon sea salt
- ¼ teaspoon paprika

Instructions:

1. Preheat oven to 375°F (190°C).
2. Toss sweet potato slices with olive oil and seasonings.
3. Arrange on a baking sheet and bake for 15–20 minutes.

Calories: 160 kcal per serving

Cooking Tip:

- **Use a mandoline slicer** for evenly thin chips.

7. Crunchy Kale Chips

A low-calorie, high-fiber snack that supports fat loss.

Ingredients:

- 1 cup kale leaves
- 1 teaspoon olive oil
- ½ teaspoon sea salt
- ¼ teaspoon garlic powder

Instructions:

1. Preheat oven to 350°F (175°C).
2. Toss kale leaves with olive oil and seasonings.
3. Spread on a baking sheet and bake for 10–12 minutes.

Calories: 110 kcal per serving

Cooking Tip:

- **Massage kale with olive oil** before baking to prevent burning.

8. Almond Butter and Apple Slices

A simple, nutritious snack with fiber and healthy fats.

Ingredients:

- 1 small apple, sliced
- 1 tablespoon almond butter

Instructions:

1. Spread almond butter onto apple slices and enjoy.

Calories: 180 kcal

Cooking Tip:

- **Use unsweetened almond butter** for maximum health benefits.

9. Cucumber Hummus Bites

A refreshing, high-fiber snack that aids digestion.

Ingredients:

- ½ cucumber, sliced
- ¼ cup hummus

Instructions:

1. Spread hummus on each cucumber slice and serve.

Calories: 120 kcal

Cooking Tip:

- **Sprinkle with paprika for added flavor and metabolism boost.**

10. Zesty Lemon Chia Pudding

A fiber-packed, gut-friendly snack for digestion and satiety.

Ingredients:

- 1 cup unsweetened almond milk
- 2 tablespoons chia seeds
- 1 teaspoon honey
- ½ teaspoon lemon zest

Instructions:

1. Mix all ingredients and refrigerate overnight.
2. Serve chilled.

Calories: 180 kcal

Cooking Tip:

- **Chia seeds expand in liquid**, making this snack very filling.

CHAPTER 8: BELLY-FLAT DESSERTS

You don't have to give up desserts to achieve your weight loss goals! The key is to choose natural, low-sugar, high-nutrient options that won't spike blood sugar or cause cravings. These 10 belly-flat desserts are packed with healthy fats, fiber, and metabolism-boosting ingredients while satisfying your sweet tooth without guilt.

1. Dark Chocolate Avocado Mousse

A creamy, nutrient-dense dessert packed with healthy fats and antioxidants.

Ingredients:

- ½ ripe avocado
- 2 tablespoons unsweetened cocoa powder
- 1 teaspoon honey or maple syrup
- ½ teaspoon vanilla extract
- ¼ teaspoon cinnamon

Instructions:

1. Blend all ingredients until smooth.
2. Chill in the fridge for 20 minutes before serving.

Calories: 180 kcal per serving

Cooking Tip:

- **Top with crushed nuts or cacao nibs** for added texture.

2. Baked Apple Cinnamon Crisp

A warm, fiber-rich dessert with natural sweetness and healthy spices.

Ingredients:

- 1 apple, sliced
- 1 tablespoon rolled oats
- ½ teaspoon cinnamon
- ½ teaspoon coconut oil
- 1 teaspoon honey

Instructions:

1. Preheat oven to 375°F (190°C).
2. Toss apple slices with cinnamon and honey.

3. Top with oats and coconut oil, then bake for 15–20 minutes.

Calories: 160 kcal per serving

Cooking Tip:

- **Use Granny Smith apples** for a lower-sugar option.

3. Protein-Packed Chia Seed Pudding

A creamy, high-fiber dessert that promotes digestion and keeps you full.

Ingredients:

- 1 cup unsweetened almond milk
- 2 tablespoons chia seeds
- ½ teaspoon vanilla extract
- 1 teaspoon honey
- ½ teaspoon cinnamon

Instructions:

1. Mix all ingredients and let sit in the fridge overnight.

2. Stir before serving and enjoy chilled.

Calories: 180 kcal per serving

Cooking Tip:

- **Top with fresh berries for extra fiber and flavor.**

4. Coconut Flour Brownies

A grain-free, low-sugar brownie that satisfies chocolate cravings.

Ingredients:

- ¼ cup coconut flour
- ¼ cup unsweetened cocoa powder
- 2 eggs
- ¼ cup melted coconut oil
- 2 tablespoons honey
- ½ teaspoon baking powder

Instructions:

1. Preheat oven to 350°F (175°C).
2. Mix all ingredients and pour into a greased baking dish.

3. Bake for 15–20 minutes.

Calories: 220 kcal per serving

Cooking Tip:

- **Let cool completely before slicing** for a fudgy texture.

5. Almond Butter Banana Ice Cream

A dairy-free, sugar-free ice cream alternative that's rich in potassium and healthy fats.

Ingredients:

- 1 frozen banana
- 1 tablespoon almond butter
- ½ teaspoon cinnamon

Instructions:

1. Blend all ingredients until smooth.
2. Freeze for 10 minutes before serving.

Calories: 190 kcal per serving

Cooking Tip:

- **Add a dash of vanilla extract for extra flavor.**

6. Lemon Coconut Energy Bars

A no-bake dessert loaded with fiber, protein, and healthy fats.

Ingredients:

- ½ cup shredded coconut
- ¼ cup almond flour
- 1 tablespoon honey
- 1 teaspoon lemon zest
- ½ teaspoon vanilla extract

Instructions:

1. Mix all ingredients and press into a dish.
2. Refrigerate for 1 hour, then slice into bars.

Calories: 160 kcal per bar

Cooking Tip:

- **Store in the fridge for up to a week** for a quick sweet treat.

7. Blueberry Almond Crumble

A warm, antioxidant-rich dessert with natural sweetness.

Ingredients:

- ½ cup blueberries
- 2 tablespoons almond flour
- 1 teaspoon coconut oil
- ½ teaspoon cinnamon

Instructions:

1. Preheat oven to 350°F (175°C).
2. Toss blueberries with cinnamon and coconut oil.
3. Top with almond flour and bake for 10 minutes.

Calories: 140 kcal per serving

Cooking Tip:

- **Pair with Greek yogurt for extra protein.**

8. Cinnamon-Spiced Poached Pears

A light, digestion-friendly dessert with natural sweetness.

Ingredients:

- 1 pear, halved
- 1 cup water
- ½ teaspoon cinnamon
- 1 teaspoon honey

Instructions:

1. Simmer pear halves in water, honey, and cinnamon for 15 minutes.
2. Serve warm.

Calories: 130 kcal per serving

Cooking Tip:

- **Use ripe pears for the best natural sweetness.**

9. Matcha Green Tea Frozen Yogurt

A probiotic-rich frozen dessert that boosts metabolism.

Ingredients:

- ½ cup Greek yogurt
- 1 teaspoon matcha green tea powder
- 1 teaspoon honey

Instructions:

1. Mix all ingredients and freeze for 30 minutes.
2. Serve cold.

Calories: 120 kcal per serving

Cooking Tip:

- **Matcha contains EGCG, a compound that promotes fat burning.**

10. Honey-Sweetened Mango Sorbet

A refreshing, naturally sweet dessert with vitamin C.

Ingredients:

- 1 cup frozen mango chunks
- 1 teaspoon honey
- ½ teaspoon lemon juice

Instructions:

1. Blend all ingredients until smooth.
2. Freeze for 15 minutes before serving.

Calories: 140 kcal per serving

Cooking Tip:

- **Use fresh mango for a richer flavor.**

CHAPTER 9: 7-DAY ZERO BELLY MEAL PLAN

Following a structured meal plan eliminates guesswork, making it easier to stay consistent, lose belly fat, and maintain energy levels. This 7-day Zero Belly meal plan is designed to provide balanced nutrition with lean proteins, fiber, healthy fats, and anti-inflammatory foods to promote digestion, metabolism, and fat loss.

Each day includes:
A metabolism-boosting morning drink
A protein-rich breakfast
A light yet satisfying lunch
A nutrient-packed dinner
Healthy snacks and desserts

DAY 1

Morning Drink:

Lemon-Ginger Fat Flush Water

Breakfast:

Avocado and Smoked Salmon on Whole-Grain Toast

Lunch:

Zesty Grilled Chicken and Kale Salad

Dinner:

Miso-Glazed Cod with Steamed Greens

Snack:

Nutty Trail Mix with Dark Chocolate

Dessert:

Baked Apple Cinnamon Crisp

DAY 2

Morning Drink:

Green Tea Metabolism Booster

Breakfast:

Blueberry Protein Pancakes

Lunch:

Quinoa and Black Bean Power Bowl

Dinner:

Garlic-Lemon Grilled Chicken with Roasted Veggies

Snack:

Cucumber Hummus Bites

Dessert:

Dark Chocolate Avocado Mousse

DAY 3

Morning Drink:

Turmeric Golden Milk

Breakfast:

Zero Belly Overnight Oats with Berries

Lunch:

Spicy Shrimp and Avocado Wrap

Dinner:

Spiced Lentil and Cauliflower Curry

Snack:

Almond Butter and Apple Slices

Dessert:

Coconut Flour Brownies

DAY 4

Morning Drink:

Chilled Hibiscus and Mint Tea

Breakfast:

Sweet Potato and Spinach Breakfast Hash

Lunch:

Mediterranean Grilled Chicken Pita

Dinner:

Zucchini Noodles with Pesto and Grilled Chicken

Snack:

Avocado Deviled Eggs

Dessert:

Lemon Coconut Energy Bars

DAY 5

Morning Drink:

Kiwi and Spinach Belly-Blast Smoothie

Breakfast:

Scrambled Egg Whites with Avocado

Lunch:

Roasted Sweet Potato and Hummus Bowl

Dinner:

Ginger Soy Salmon with Steamed Bok Choy

Snack:

No-Bake Protein Bites

Dessert:

Matcha Green Tea Frozen Yogurt

DAY 6

Morning Drink:

Coconut Water Electrolyte Refresher

Breakfast:

Protein-Packed Peanut Butter Banana Smoothie

Lunch:

Chickpea and Spinach Stuffed Peppers

Dinner:

Hearty Lentil and Kale Stew

Snack:

Crunchy Kale Chips

Dessert:

Cinnamon-Spiced Poached Pears

DAY 7

Morning Drink:

Lemon-Ginger Fat Flush Water

Breakfast:

Greek Yogurt and Walnut Power Bowl

Lunch:

Cucumber and Avocado Sushi Rolls

Dinner:

Thai Basil Shrimp Stir-Fry

Snack:

Baked Sweet Potato Chips

Dessert:

Honey-Sweetened Mango Sorbet

How to Follow the 7-Day Meal Plan for Maximum Results

1. Stick to whole, minimally processed foods— avoid refined carbs and sugars.
2. Stay hydrated: drink at least 8 cups of water per day.
3. Balance your portions: ensure each meal has protein, fiber, and healthy fats.
4. Listen to your body: eat when hungry and stop when full.
5. Prep meals in advance: batch-cook proteins and store snacks for convenience.

CHAPTER 10: CONCLUSION & LONG-TERM SUCCESS STRATEGIES

Congratulations! You've reached the final chapter of the Zero Belly Wonder Cookbook, but this is just the beginning of your journey toward sustainable fat loss, a healthier gut, and lasting well-being. This chapter will provide long-term strategies to help you maintain your results, build healthy habits, and make this lifestyle effortless.

1. The Zero Belly Lifestyle: A Long-Term Approach

This cookbook isn't about temporary dieting, it's about adopting a way of eating that fuels your body, supports digestion, and prevents belly fat accumulation.

To make the Zero Belly approach sustainable, focus on: Whole, minimally processed foods :– Stick to real ingredients, lean proteins, healthy fats, and fiber-rich meals.

Balanced macronutrients :– Every meal should contain protein, fiber, and healthy fats to stabilize blood sugar and reduce cravings.

Hydration :– Drinking enough water and detoxifying drinks prevents bloating, keeps digestion smooth, and enhances metabolism.

Regular movement :– You don't need to overtrain; just move daily with walking, stretching, or strength training.

Mindful eating – Listen to your hunger cues and avoid stress eating or emotional snacking.

2. How to Keep Belly Fat Off for Good

Prioritize Fiber & Protein

- Fiber keeps digestion moving smoothly and prevents bloating.
- Protein builds lean muscle, burns fat, and stabilizes blood sugar.
- Include at least 20-30g of protein per meal and fiber from vegetables, fruits, and whole grains.

Avoid Sugar & Refined Carbs

- Excess sugar leads to belly fat storage, insulin spikes, and cravings.
- Stick to natural sweeteners like honey, maple syrup, or fruit in moderation.

Eat More Healthy Fats

- Good fats like avocado, olive oil, nuts, and seeds suppress appetite and support metabolism.
- Ditch trans fats (found in fried and processed foods) to prevent inflammation.

Drink Smart

- Limit sugary drinks and alcohol—they contribute to belly fat.
- Hydration is key! Drink at least 8 cups of water daily.
- Use herbal teas, detox waters, and smoothies to keep digestion healthy.

Sleep & Stress Management

- Poor sleep leads to increased cravings and stress-related weight gain.
- Aim for 7-9 hours of quality sleep per night.
- Manage stress with meditation, deep breathing, or journaling.

3. Meal Prep & Smart Grocery Shopping Tips

Plan Your Meals in Advance

- Write out a weekly meal plan (use the **7-day plan** as a guide).
- Prepare protein sources and snacks ahead of time.

Stock Your Kitchen with Zero Belly Essentials

- Protein: Chicken, fish, eggs, tofu, Greek yogurt.
- Healthy Fats: Avocados, olive oil, nuts, seeds.
- Fiber-Rich Foods: Leafy greens, quinoa, oats, lentils.
- Low-Glycemic Fruits: Berries, apples, pears.
- Metabolism-Boosting Spices: Turmeric, cinnamon, cayenne.

Avoid "Trigger Foods" That Cause Weight Gain

- Sugary snacks, white bread, soda, and fried foods shouldn't be in your pantry.
- Stick to whole, natural foods that nourish your body.

4. Simple Swaps for Everyday Eating

Making small, consistent changes helps sustain fat loss without feeling restricted.

- Instead of white rice → Cauliflower rice or quinoa.

- Instead of white bread → Whole-grain or almond flour bread.

- Instead of soda → Lemon-infused water or iced herbal tea.

- Instead of sugar-filled desserts → Dark chocolate or fruit-based treats.

- Instead of fried snacks → Baked kale chips or roasted chickpeas.
- By making these simple adjustments, you'll naturally maintain a leaner waistline without feeling deprived.

5. Staying on Track: Overcoming Challenges & Plateaus

What to Do When You Hit a Weight Loss Plateau

- Increase fiber intake to support digestion.
- Drink more detox teas and infused waters to reduce bloating.
- Adjust portion sizes if you're eating more than needed.
- Add more protein to balance blood sugar and burn fat.

How to Handle Cravings

- Drink water first: cravings are often due to dehydration.
- Eat healthy fats like nuts or avocado to reduce hunger.
- Choose fruit instead of processed sweets for a natural sugar fix.

How to Eat Out Without Gaining Belly Fat

- Choose protein and veggies over carb-heavy dishes.
- Avoid sugary sauces-opt for lemon, olive oil, or vinaigrette dressings.
- Control portion sizes by eating half and saving the rest.

6. Your Zero Belly Journey: What's Next?

Celebrate Progress, Not Perfection

- Focus on how you feel:- better digestion, more energy, improved sleep.
- Take progress pictures and measurements rather than relying only on weight.

Stay Consistent & Flexible

- You don't have to be perfect-aim for 80% clean eating while allowing treats in moderation.
- If you slip up, get back on track at the next meal-don't wait for Monday!

Find Joy in the Process

- Cooking should be enjoyable, not stressful. Experiment with new flavors, spices, and meal variations.
- Find an accountability partner or meal-prep with friends to stay motivated.

Make This a Lifestyle, Not a Diet

- Zero Belly eating isn't about restriction—it's about fueling your body with the right foods for long-term health.
- Keep learning, trying new recipes, and listening to your body as you continue this journey.

CONCLUSION

You now have all the tools you need to burn fat, improve digestion, and maintain a lean, healthy body without deprivation. By incorporating the recipes, meal plans, and strategies in this book, you'll be able to build a sustainable, enjoyable way of eating that promotes lasting health and wellness.

Whether your goal is shedding belly fat, feeling more energized, or simply improving your diet, the Zero Belly Wonder Cookbook is designed to support you every step of the way.

Your journey to a healthier, stronger, and more confident.

BONUS: RESOURCES & FREQUENTLY ASKED QUESTIONS

Q: Can I modify the meal plan for vegetarian or dairy-free diets?

A: Yes! Simply swap lean meats for tofu, tempeh, or legumes and use dairy-free yogurt or plant-based milk.

Q: How soon will I see results?
A: Many people notice reduced bloating and more energy within the first few days. Significant fat loss depends on consistency and lifestyle habits.

Q: Can I still enjoy treats occasionally?
A: Absolutely! Balance is key enjoy healthier dessert alternatives or occasional indulgences in moderation.

Q: Do I have to count calories?
A: No! If you focus on whole, unprocessed foods and listen to your hunger signals, you'll naturally eat the right amount.

Printed in Great Britain
by Amazon

62313948R00077